GHOST BEHIND THE STARS

Chris Powling

Illustrated by Michael Reid

How can I stop the ghost who's spooking out our local TV studio?

A & C Black • London

The comix series ...

Aargh, it's an Alien! · Karen Wallace
Agent Spike and the Vegetables of Doom · Mark Burgess
Archie's Amazing Game · Michael Hardcastle
Arf and the Greedy Grabber · Philip Wooderson
Arf and the Metal Detector · Philip Wooderson
Arf and the Three Dogs · Philip Wooderson
Freddy's Fox · Anthony Masters
A Ghost Behind the Stars · Chris Powling
The Goose Who Knew Too Much · Peter Utton
Henry's Magic Powers · Peter Utton
Hot Air · Anthony Masters
Jack's Tree · Georgia Byng
Joker · Anthony Masters
Mr Potts the Potty Teacher · Colin West
Monster School · Garry Kilworth
The Planet Machine · Steve Bowkett
Please Don't Eat my Sister! · Caroline Pitcher
Sam's Dream · Michael Hardcastle
Uncle Tom's Pterodactyl · Colin West
Yikes, it's a Yeti! · Karen Wallace

First published in paperback 2002. Reprinted 2004
First published in hardback 2002 by A & C Black Publishers Ltd
37 Soho Square, London, W1D 3QZ
www.acblack.com

Text copyright © 2002 Chris Powling
Illustrations copyright © 2002 Michael Reid

The rights of Chris Powling and Michael Reid to be identified
as author and illustrator of this work have been asserted by them in
accordance with the Copyrights, Designs and Patents Act 1988.

ISBN 0-7136-6102-X

A CIP catalogue for this book is available from the
British Library.

Printed and bound in Spain by G. Z. Printek, Bilbao

CHAPTER ONE

It was Grandpa who mentioned the ghost. Tessa stared at him, wide-eyed. So did Tom, her twin brother.

Was he piling up the suspense... or just nervous about scaring them witless?

4

Eventually, he brushed a speck of dust from his uniform and straightened his official cap.

Tessa and Tom looked at the words on the badge. They didn't feel very secure right now. Right now, what they felt was... ghostly.

Grandpa cleared his throat.

Sometimes, I can hear him singing, you know.

Singing?

Tom frowned.

Tom and Tessa shifted in their seats. Grandpa had always been a bit of a tease. But he seemed deadly serious now.

Suddenly, the cubby-hole he used as an office felt a whole lot spookier.

Grandpa pointed at the wall behind them.

Each famous face was supplied with an autograph...
all signed for Grandpa personally.

All except one, that is.

There it was: an old-fashioned figure, dressed in old-fashioned clothes, who'd been snapped by an old-fashioned camera. Even the signature looked old-fashioned. In neat, swirly writing it said:

Unforgettably yours
Max Benbow

Tessa gave a shrug.

Grandpa sniffed.

Max Benbow? Who on earth is Max Benbow?

Well, he shouldn't be on earth at all, Tess. He's been dead for fifty–odd years. Trouble is, I'm not sure he's ever left us.

You mean he's still alive?

Not alive, no. Just sort of... well, hanging around to haunt us.

People queued for hours when they knew Max Benbow was appearing. Hundreds and hundreds of them.

Mind you, that's not very many compared with a television audience today – THE BOB AND CYNTHIA SHOW, for instance.

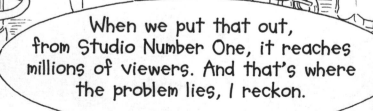

When we put that out, from Studio Number One, it reaches millions of viewers. And that's where the problem lies, I reckon.

Exactly.

That's assuming you're not making this up. Maybe you've been kidding us all along about this ghost of Max Benbow!

Grandpa cupped a hand to his ear.

Have I, Tess?

He was listening hard.

And that's when they heard it, too. Early in the morning, they could be pretty sure they would be alone in this strange, security-guarded, monster of a place. So how come there was music — live music — hanging eerily in the air?

Someone, deep in the building, was playing an old-fashioned tune on a piano.

CHAPTER TWO

Luckily, Grandpa knew exactly what to do. Jingling his keys, he rose to his feet.

There's only one cure for the heebie-jeebies. We've got to keep ourselves busy. Let's get the studio sorted out for this morning's transmission.

STUDIOS

Can we do the fixing, Grandpa?

This was true.

Grandpa had worked at the TV Station for years. During his time there, he'd become an expert on everything that happened there. According to Peter McHugh, the famous Director of Programmes, Grandpa was the best all-rounder on his staff.

So, ghost or no ghost, they felt pretty confident as they hurried along the corridor to Studio Number One. This had an odd sort of layout, really, being half a sitting-room and half a performing-area with a newsdesk tucked snugly between the two.

As usual, there were four cameras in position. Two of them faced Bob and Cynthia's legendary sofa.

Off you go, then... one switch is down here on the autocue and one up here on the viewfinder. And you'd better unlock their pedestals so they can tilt and pan and shift up and down.

Leave them on the test-card for now, Tom.

Are we preparing for full sound and vision? If so, we'll need back-up mikes.

Smart lad.

Next, they moved to the control room. Grandpa often called it 'the gallery' and it was easy to see why.

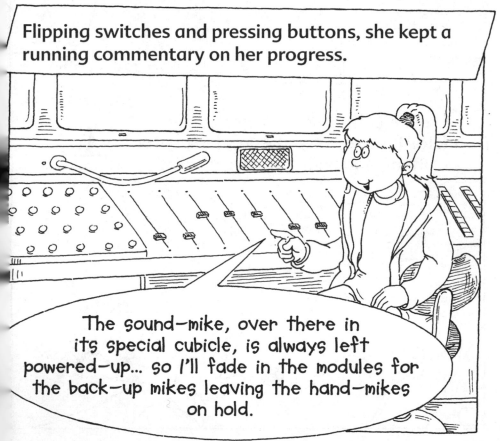

Now it was Tessa's turn to show off.

Flipping switches and pressing buttons, she kept a running commentary on her progress.

The sound-mike, over there in its special cubicle, is always left powered-up... so I'll fade in the modules for the back-up mikes leaving the hand-mikes on hold.

Everything was ready for transmission now. Having been so busy it was no wonder the twins had forgotten about Max Benbow, until...

Grandpa coughed awkwardly.

Well, I do have an idea...it involves making a tape, you see — a videotape of Max Benbow in action. Once that's safely in the can, and ready for broadcasting at any time, why should he feel threatened by THE BOB AND CYNTHIA SHOW?

How are we supposed to film a ghost?

We don't.

What?

We make a film of me instead — dressed up as Max Benbow — performing some of his favourite routines. He'd never dream of sabotaging a personal tribute!

Tessa put a hand on his arm.

Are you really... well... good enough to play the part of Max Benbow?

Good enough? Of course I'm not good enough, Tess. The man had a touch of genius! But when we've edited the tape and put in a bit of techno—wizardry, even the old boy himself won't be able to tell the difference.

He was beaming at them now.

And they didn't have a better idea.

From somewhere down by the scenery dock, they caught an echo of thin, ghostly laughter.

Ha he, hee hee, hoo hoo.

CHAPTER THREE

Halfway home, the twins paused for breath. All round them stretched the bridges and walkways of the estate where they lived — like a futuristic city, Mum always said.

But it was spooks, not scenery, that gripped them.

I've heard of ghostwriters, but not a ghost performer filmed on videotape.

It won't be a ghost performer, will it? Just Grandpa pretending to be a performer. I only hope it's enough to satisfy Max, that's all.

Suppose it isn't?

Then the TV station is done for, Tom. People grumble already that it's too small and remote to survive. THE BOB AND CYNTHIA SHOW is its only lifeline, they say.

Imagine the effect of a series of ghostly glitches or a haunting—or—two disguised as technical failure... everyone will be out of a job, including Grandpa!

Over the western horizon hung a low, brooding bank of cloud.

That's all we need. Weirdness and bad weather is a scary combination!

Very televisual, though.

You're right, sis. With an outside broadcast unit, we could set up a tracking shot...

Tom shaped a viewfinder with his hands.

He traced a camera angle in the air.

Tessa watched him, fascinated.

There's our opening sequence! All we need now is a title! What shall we call this programme of ours, Tom?

Well, how about...

Yes?

A GHOST BEHIND THE STARS?

CHAPTER FOUR

Grandpa loved it. He rolled the words over his tongue as if he relished the very sound of them.

A GHOST BEHIND THE STARS. That's perfect, kids — it hits just the right note.

He was warming them up for his pep-talk, they realised.

They'd heard it a hundred times. But never before while Grandpa was dressed as Max Benbow — in a pork-pie hat and a suit patterned in bold, black-and-white checks.

He lowered his voice almost to a whisper.

Okay, let's remember that this studio is nothing to be scared of.

Tom was on camera today.

Now... these tiny red dots on either side of the viewfinder are there to tell me when I'm actually on air, right?

To check this, he zoomed in, smooth and tight.

What Tessa saw, on her monitor in the gallery, was Grandpa's trick with the ten pence piece. He flipped the coin over his knuckles in time with his own singing.

Every time it rains, it rains pennies from heaven. Don't you know each cloud contains pennies from heaven...

Then, as he flicked his wrist, the coin vanished till —
with another flick — it dropped from his nose or eyes
or mouth.

At this point, Tom pulled back the camera to show Grandpa's old-fashioned umbrella opening the right way up.

Grandpa was delighted when they played the tape back.

Of course, that tune wasn't written for Max, kids – not till long after he was dead, in fact. Otherwise, I performed it exactly as he'd have done.

Also, they could see the trouble Grandpa had taken to lay it out in a professional way:

Slug: N/Hello Read
Writer: Grandpa 2.2.01 (page 201)
Last: Rowley Tessa
Rundown: 6.30 Fri
Printed by: Grandpa

———————————————

Roll titles__ C __   (Titles)

Cam __ Me __   (Grandpa)
Good morning. It's Sunday,
February 4th. Welcome to
City TV and a special
one-off programme. Our
presenter is the great
Max Benbow...

Their presenter was Max Benbow, too... or someone as close as Grandpa could make him.

Whether dancing, singing, card-tricking, playing the piano or simply talking to camera, his performance amazed them.

Don't you believe it, son. Max had that extra touch of genius.

Grandpa smiled wryly.

And it makes all the difference in the world, you know... the difference between a superstar and a security guard, for instance.

But he still managed a wink at Max's photograph. It stood out amongst all the shots of modern TV stars on the wall.

Okay, old–timer? On Saturday, there's THE BOB AND CYNTHIA SHOW as usual. After that, on Sunday, we'll be laying your stroppy old spirit to rest...

By now, Tom and Tessa couldn't wait.

CHAPTER FIVE

That night it was hard to sleep. But it wasn't Sunday's recording that bothered them. Why should they worry when they knew how well they'd been trained?

What had changed was the weather.

At suppertime, snow began falling. Down it came with a steady, world-smothering heaviness. Before sunrise next morning, their high-rise estate was cut off from the city and the city was cut off from everywhere else. Including, of course, the TV station.

Tessa stared at Tom in dismay.

Winter-proofed from head to foot, the twins crossed the ice-bound bridges and frozen walk-ways of the estate.

On the TV screen in the entrance lobby, Grandpa glowered down at them with the face of Max Benbow.

So you've got here at last, I'd almost given up on you!

The twins had already decided.

They'd broken into a run.

At the vision-mixer, Tessa took special care to press the right buttons. She spoke into the phone in her most grown-up voice.

Hello, is that Central Control?
This is satellite station CITY TV.
We've got a signal for you.
Are you seeing it?
We've switched it out to line...

No problems, CITY TV.
Good to see the weather hasn't knocked you out.
Over to you for transmission, fading up the vision to line...

They were on the air.

Tom's opening shot, after the titles, was a close-up of a pair of tap-dancing feet.

They twinkled across the studio floor with dazzling deftness and speed.

After this, the twins were too busy to be nervous —
Tom behind the camera and Tessa at the desk — with
Grandpa, in his Max Benbow outfit, singing, clowning,
and playing the piano like someone born to be top of
the bill.

She almost froze at the desk.

Only Grandpa's training kept her on track. The final credits were rolling, cunningly framed by Tom against a long-shot of the snow-stricken city, before Tessa found she could breath normally again.

The phone rang almost at once.

Central Control. We're off you now.

Thanks.

Great little programme that, by the way. Had a nice, old-fashioned feel to it. I reckon it could land an award. Where did you find the old guy?

Oh, he hangs around here.

I'd put him on contract if I were you. He's got something really special about him!

You could say that, yes.

Tessa put down the phone.

Still shaking, she met Tom at the gallery door. From the shock on his face, it was clear he realised what had happened.

That was him, wasn't it?
We ended up with a ghost performer, after all. In which case, where's Grandpa?

Locked in his office, I bet.
To keep him out of the way while the real star of the show...

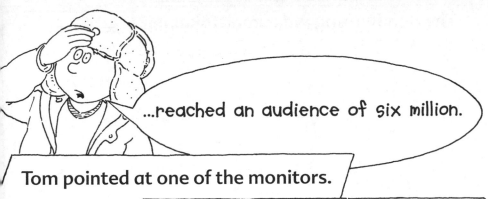

...reached an audience of six million.

Tom pointed at one of the monitors.

There, across the test-card, it said:

After all, Grandpa was the best all-rounder at CITY TV.